W9-DBO-227

LOAN COLLECTION

SUZANNE FISCHER | Early Morning Warm-UP (P)

Professional Photographers of America

Volume VIII 2005

Published by

MARATHON PRESS • MARATHON PUBLICATIONS • MARATHON INTERNET SERVICES

Bienvenidos a la edición del año 2005 del Libro de préstamos de Professional Photographers of America. Estas imágenes fueron elegidos por los miembros del jurado homologados por PPA en el marco del Concurso Internacional del año 2005 como "lo mejor de lo mejor" de entre miles de propuestas. Estos trabajos que se expondrán en la Exhibición fotográfica de PPA en 2005 en los EE.UU. representan un nivel de calidad en cuanto a la creatividad y técnica a la que todo fotógrafo en cualquier lugar puede aspirar.

En nombre de la Junta Directiva quiero expresar mis felicitaciones a los autores de estas destacadas obras artísticas y mi agradecimiento a todos aquellos que han hecho posible este libro: el Comité de Exposiciones Fotográficas, los miembros del jurado internacional, los voluntarios y el personal de PPA y a Marathon Press.

Espero que esta colección sirva de fuente de inspiración a fotógrafos en cualquier lugar y como rica herramienta formativa a compartir con los consumidores que aprecian el arte de la fotografía.

Ann K. Monteith

Ann K. Monteith
CPP,M.Photog.Cr.,A-ASP,HonA-Asp,ABI,API
Presidente de PPA 2005-2006

Nous sommes ravis de vous présenter l'édition 2005 du livre de la collection de prêts de Professional Photographers of America. Ces images ont été sélectionnées lors du 2005 International Judging par un jury approuvé par PPA avec pour seul mot d'ordre de ne choisir que « la crème de la crème » parmi les milliers d'images proposées. Ces images, présentées lors de l'exposition Imaging USA de PPA en 2006, symbolisent l'excellence dans les domaines de la créativité et de la technique, à laquelle aspire tout photographe.

Au nom du Conseil d'Administration, je tiens à féliciter tous les artistes auteurs de ces images exceptionnelles et à remercier ceux et celles qui ont fait de ce livre une réalité : le Photographic Exhibitions Committee, le jury international, les bénévoles et le personnel de PPA, ainsi que Marathon Press.

Que cette collection devienne à la fois une source d'inspiration pour les photographes du monde entier et une ressource éducative à partager avec les hommes et les femmes qui savent apprécier l'art de la photographie.

Ann K. Monteith

Ann K. Monteith
CPP,M.Photog.Cr.,A-ASP,HonA-Asp,ABI,API
Président de PPA 2005-2006

Willkommen zur Ausgabe 2005 des Loan Books von Professional Photographers of America. Diese Bilder wurden von den PPA-Juroren im Rahmen des internationalen Wettbewerbs des Jahres 2005 als „die Besten der Besten" unter Tausenden von Einsendungen ausgewählt. Diese auf der Fotoausstellung der PPA im Jahr 2006 in den Vereinigten Staaten auszustellenden Bilder spiegeln das Niveau der hervorragendsten Leistungen im Sinne der Kreativität und der Technik wider, die sich ein jeder Fotograf nur wünschen kann.

Im Namen des Vorstandes beglückwünsche ich alle Autoren dieser ganz besonderen Kunstwerke und möchte mich bei allen bedanken, die dieses Buch ermöglicht haben: dem Ausschuss für Fotografieausstellungen, den internationalen Juroren, den freiwilligen Helfern und Mitarbeitern der PPA und bei Marathon Press.

Ich hoffe, diese Sammlung dient allen Fotografen als Inspiration und reche Weiterbildungsquelle, um sie mit Kunden, die die Kunst der Fotografie schätzen, zu teilen.

Ann K. Monteith

Ann K. Monteith
CPP,M.Photog.Cr.,A-ASP,HonA-Asp,ABI,API
Vorsitzender der PPA 2005-2006

全米プロ写真家協会の2005年版貸出書籍へようこそお越しいただきました。これらの画像は、2005年全米プロ写真家協会の国際審査で、何千ものエントリーから「最優秀」として全米プロ写真家協会認定の審査員によって選ばれました。全米プロ写真家協会の2006年イメージング USA 展示会で展示されるこれらの画像は、あらゆる写真家の方々が求める創造性と技能の優秀レベルを表しています。

全米プロ写真家協会の理事会を代表して、このような素晴らしい芸術作品の制作者にお祝いを述べると共に、この本を世に送り出すことを可能にしてくださった写真展示委員会、国際審査員、全米プロ写真家協会のボランティアの方々とスタッフ、ならびにマラソンプレスに対して感謝いたします。

このコレクションがあらゆる写真家の方々にインスピレーションを与え、写真芸術を鑑賞される方々と共有する豊かな教育リソースとしてお役に立つことを願っております。

Ann K. Monteith

アン K. モンテース
PPA Certified, M.Photog.Cr., A-ASP, HonA-ASP, ABI, API
2005-2006 PPA 会長

歡迎閱覽2005年版的 Professional Photographers of America's Loan book（專業攝影出借書籍）。這些照片都是由 PPA-Approved Jurors 在2005年 International Judging（國際評審）幾千張作品中挑選出來的"精品中的精品"。這些照片，會在 PPA's 2006 Imaging USA Exhibition（2006年美國PPA攝影展）上展出，代表當今世界攝影師的卓越的創造和新技術。

我代表董事會，我祝賀這些傑出藝術作品的作者們，以及感謝爲出版這本書做出貢獻的人們：the Photographic Exhibition Committee, the International Jurors, PPA職員者和工作人員還有 Marathon Press。

希望這本專集能夠鼓舞世界的攝影家們，並給那些欣賞攝影藝術的消費者提供豐富的教材。

Ann K. Monteith

Ann K. Monteith（安 K.曼麗絲）
PPA Certified, M.Photog.Cr., A-ASP, HonA-ASP, ABI, API
2005-2006 PPA 會長

Volume VIII 2005

Marathon

Marathon Press • Marathon Publications • Marathon Internet Services

1500 Square Turn Boulevard, Norfolk, Nebraska 68701

(402) 371-5040 • Fax (402) 371-9382 • **(800) 228-0629** E-MAIL: contact@marathonpress.com www.marathonpress.com

ISBN: 1-893696-38-3

©Marathon Press, 2005 All rights reserved. No part of this book may be reproduced, translated, stored in a retrieval system, or transmitted by any means, without prior permission in writing from the publisher.

PRESIDENT'S MESSAGE

Welcome to the 2005 edition of the Professional Photographers of America's Loan book. These images were selected by PPA-Approved Jurors at the 2005 International Judging as the "best of the best" from the thousands of entries. These images, displayed at PPA's 2006 Imaging USA Exhibition, represent a standard of excellence in creativity and technique to which photographers everywhere can aspire.

On behalf of the Board of Directors, I congratulate the makers of these outstanding artworks and offer thanks to those who made this book possible: the Photographic Exhibition Committee, the International Jurors, PPA volunteers and staff, and Marathon Press.

May this collection serve as an inspiration to photographers everywhere and as a rich educational resource to share with consumers who appreciate the art of photography.

Ann K. Monteith

Ann K. Monteith
CPP,M.Photog.Cr.,A-ASP,HonA-ASP,ABI,API
2005-2006 PPA President

Nous sommes ravis de vous présenter les meilleures publications annuelles des Photographes Professionnels d'Amérique, les PPA!

Chaque année, lorsque nous nous occupons de la publication des livres *PPA Loan Collection* et *PPA Showcase*, nous nous émerveillons du niveau de l'expression créative et de l'expertise présentés dans ces volumes. Pour ces seules raisons, le personnel de Marathon est particulièrement fier d'être associé à un projet d'un tel prestige. Nous sommes également très conscients de l'importance du Concours International d'Images annuel de PPA (International Print Competition) en termes de sa capacité à établir et maintenir les normes d'excellence que tout photographe dans le monde cherche à atteindre.

Nous sommes également impressionnés par le fait que l'exposition de ces images a une valeur éducative immense. En effet, lorsqu'un photographe regarde cette collection, étudie les images des livres que nous publions, ou s'implique dans le processus du concours, un apprentissage inestimable se produit.

Dès lors, Marathon tient à féliciter tous ceux et celles qui font de ce concours extraordinaire un succès, et participent à la création de cette ressource unique et vitale pour tous les photographes et les faiseurs d'images du monde entier.

Salutations distinguées,

Rex Alewel

Rex Alewel, *Éditeur*

Willkommen zu den wichtigsten jährlichen Veröffentlichungen der Professional Photographers of America!

Jedes Jahr bei der Erstellung der Veröffentlichung *PPA Loan Collection* und des Buchs *PPA Showcase* überrascht uns das hohe Niveau des kreativen Ausdrucks und das Können, das in diesen Bänden vorgestellt wird. Schon deshalb sind die Mitarbeiter von Marathon stolz darauf, an einem so renommierten Projekt beteiligt zu sein. Wir sind uns auch darüber bewusst, was der jährliche internationale Druckwettbewerb der PPA hinsichtlich der Möglichkeit, Standards des Könnens zu definieren und beizubehalten, die dann von Fotografen auf der ganzen Welt angestrebt werden können, für die Branche bedeutet.

Wir sind auch von den Lehrfähigkeiten der gedruckten Ausstellung beeindruckt. Wenn ein Fotograf die Sammlung selbst ansieht, die Bilder in dem von uns veröffentlichten Buch studiert oder den Ablauf des Wettbewerbs nachvollzieht, findet ein unschätzbarer Lernprozess statt.

Deshalb übermittelt Marathon an alle, die aus diesem außergewöhnlichen Wettbewerb einen Erfolg gemacht haben, seine Glückwünsche für die Schaffung einer einmaligen und vitalen Ressource für Fotografen und Bildkünstler allerorts.

Mit freundlichen Grüßen,

Rex Alewel

Rex Alewel, *Verleger*

¡Bienvenido a las principales publicaciones de Professional Photographers of America!

Cada año, cuando realizamos el proceso de publicación de la *Colección de Préstamos de la PPA* y del *Libro Expositor de la PPA*, nos maravilla el alto nivel de expresión creativa y habilidades técnicas presentados en estos volúmenes. Ya sólo este hecho enorgullece al personal de Marathon por poder participar en un proyecto de tanto prestigio. También somos consientes de la importancia de la competición impresa de la PPA para el sector, en cuanto a la capacidad de establecer y mantener los niveles de excelencia que los fotógrafos a nivel mundial pueden intentar alcanzar.

Estamos igualmente impresionados por las posibilidades formativas de esta exhibición impresa. Cada vez que un fotógrafo observa la colección misma, estudia las imágenes en los libros que publicamos o revisa el proceso de la competición, se desarrolla un proceso de aprendizaje inestimable.

Por ello, Marathon transmite sus felicidades a todos, que han convertido esta competición extraordinaria en un éxito, por ofrecer un recurso único y vital para los fotógrafos y artistas de las imágenes de todo el mundo.

Atentamente,

Rex Alewel

Rex Alewel, *Editor*

歡迎閱讀美國專業攝影師協會首選的年度出版物。

在每年出版 PPA 精品圖書和 PPA 展示窗圖書的過程中，我們都爲書中富有創造性的表現方法和專業水准而感到驚訝。僅此一點就使 Marathon 的職員們爲能夠工作于這樣一個高水平的作品而感到自豪。我們還意識到 PPA 每年的國際攝影評選對攝影行業意味着什么--它爲世界範圍内的攝影師建立并維護了一個共同追求的高標准。

我們還爲攝影展覽的教育價值而感動。對攝影師來説，欣賞入選的作品，研究我們的出版物中的攝影，甚至經歷整個評選過程本身都是無價的學習機會。

在本屆攝影評選中勝出的攝影師們，Marathon 祝賀你們爲世界各地的攝影師和攝影工作者們提供了一個獨特而重要的資源。

Rex Alewel

Rex Alewel 出版商

毎年恒例となっているアメリカプロ写真家協会（PPA）からの写真集へようこそ！

毎年、「PPA ローン コレクション写真集」および「PPA ショーケース写真集」の発行に当たってその作業を進める時、我々はそこに収められている作品の持つ創造性と、それらの作品の制作に用いられている専門技術のレベルの高さに感嘆せざるを得ません。Marathon Press 社のスタッフ一同は、この卓越した芸術出版プロジェクトに関与できることに誇りを感じております。同時に、毎年開催される PPA の国際大会の結果によって、世界各国の職業写真家達が目標とするべき業界の標準が書き換えられ続けているという点において、この大会がいかに意義深いものであるかということも認識しております。

さらには、一写真家が弊社出版の本写真集のページをめくる時、あるいは大会における審査過程を経験していく時、そこには常に貴重な学習のチャンスが存在しているということ、すなわち作品の一つ一つに他の写真家達を啓発していく力が秘められているということにも感銘を受けております。

Marathon Press 社では、この卓越したコンテストを成功へと導いた皆様方一人一人に、世界中の写真家および画像製作者のためのユニークかつ貴重な資源を創り出したその素晴らしい業績に対し、心からの祝福の意を表したいと思います。

Rex Alewel

Rex Alewel
発行責任者

A WORD FROM THE PUBLISHER

Welcome to PPA's Loan Collection, Volume VIII ~ 2005!

Every year, as we proceed through the process of publishing the PPA Loan Collection and PPA Showcase books, we marvel at the level of creative expression and expertise that is presented in these volumes. This alone makes the staff at Marathon proud to be associated with a project of such distinction. We also are aware of how much PPA's annual International Print Competition means to the industry in terms of its ability to set and maintain standards of excellence that photographers worldwide can seek to achieve.

We are impressed also with the capacity of the print exhibition to educate. Whenever a photographer views the collection itself, studies images in the books we publish, or goes through the process of competition, invaluable learning takes place.

So to all those who make this extraordinary competition a success, Marathon sends its congratulations on fashioning a unique and vital resource for photographers and image makers everywhere.

Sincerely,

Rex Alewel, Publisher

ALLISON ENGLISH WATKINS | Waiting For Their Gentlemen (P)

CRAIG KIENAST | Miss Leading Lines (P)

JULIE KLAASMEYER | That's Hot!!! (P)

JOHN WACKER | Focused (P)

B.C. BAGGETT | Generations of Courage (P)

LOAN COLLECTION

WAYNE TARR | Shadow Dancer (P)

LOU SZOKE | Backstage (P)

LOAN COLLECTION

LIBA COPLEN | No Greater Love (P)

MARY MORTENSEN | A Gift From God (P)

WILLIAM STEVENSON | Pixilated Pelican (P)

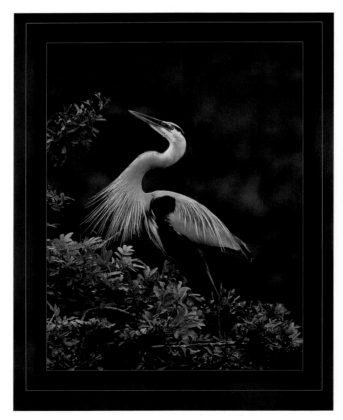

JOE CAMPANELLIE | Just Showin' Off (P)

BILLIE NICHOLSON | Dockside (P)

JENNIFER NOURSE RODMAN | Morning At Lido (P)

DONG SEOK PARK | The Mystery Of Nature (P)

JAE KWANG LEE | Love Like A Fairy Tale (P)

JO BURKHARDT | Once Upon A Time (A-EI)

JO BURKHARDT | Caffe' Bernini (A-EI)

GIGI CLARK | Remains Of The Day — A Tapestry (DP)

GIGI CLARK | It Happens All The Time (DP)

HUD ANDREWS | Beauty (P)

CARL SAATHOFF | Fire And Ice (P)

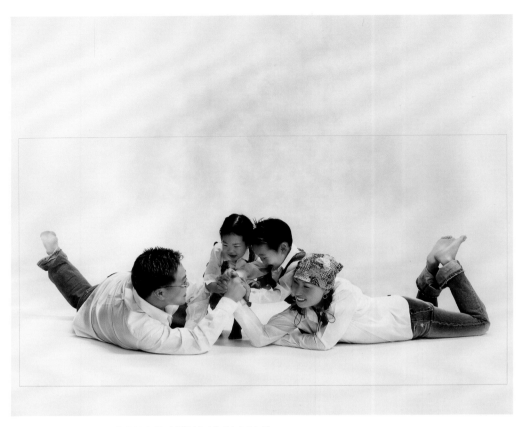

YOUNG HWAN KANG | Family's Harmony (P)

KUNIHIRO KIKUCHI | Tsunokawa Family (P)

DAVID HEINZELMAN | Basket Pedlar (P)

DAVID HEINZELMAN | Zorba The Sheep Herder (P)

STEWART SCHULZE | Valley On Fire (P)

ROGER CAREY | Capturing Death Valley (P)

STEPHEN ABBOTT | The Family Farm (P)

RICHARD BEITZEL | The Visit (P)

BRANDON MICHAEL | Define Fashion (C)

MAZ MASHRU | Henna Lady (P)

DIXIE DOBBINS | Artistic Liberty (P)

JOHN RIDGEWAY | Arches & Angles (P)

LOLA STEWART | Strollin' On The Pier (P)

KURT WADE | Sunday In Paris (P)

K.C. MONTGOMERY | The Race (P)

JEFF JANSON | Flaxen Dance (P)

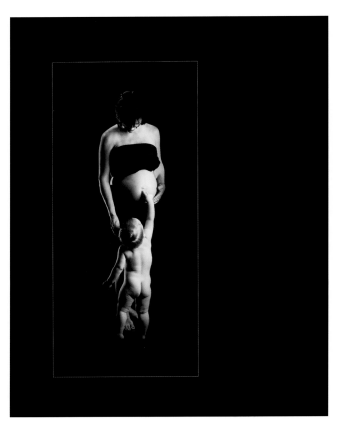

RENA BALDENEGRO | Baby Dispenser (P)

MARTHA ANNE BASS | A Flower Waiting To Bloom (P)

HYUN MO HAN | Pretty Bride (P)

GERALDINE LAGO | Modern Bride (P)

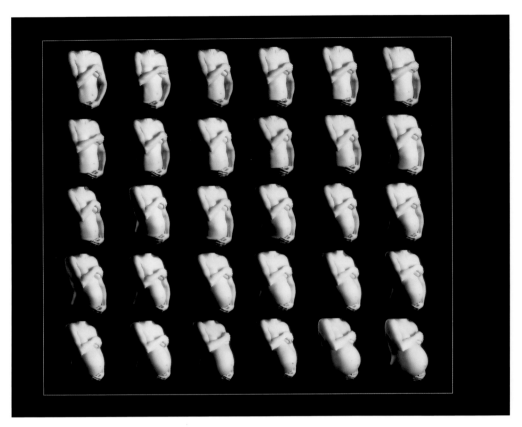

ANTHONY MARILL | Gestation (P)

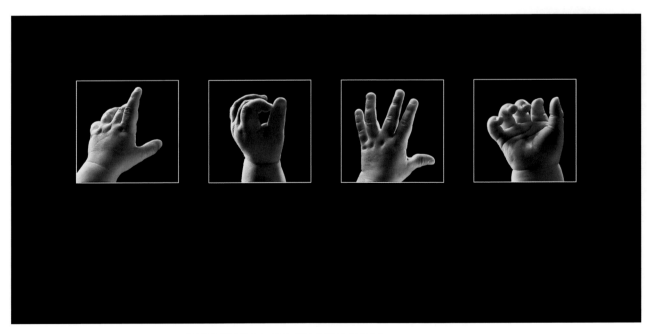

MITCHELL RICHARDSON | L-O-V-E (P)

CYNTHIA BAXTER | Mugsy (P)

CLARK MARTEN | Blast From The Past (P)

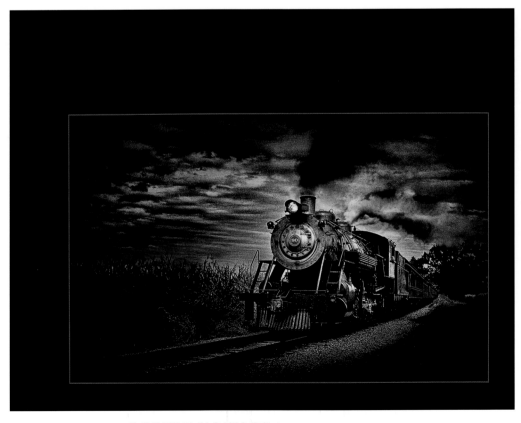

ROBERT HOWARD | Midnight Run (P)

LOAN COLLECTION

KEN WEBB | Reaching For Peace (P)

BRYAN WHITE | Divine Inspiration (P)

RICHARD LOFGREEN | Self Portrait (P)

DAVID WACKER | A Little Privacy Please! (P)

GERD HARDER | After Midnight (P)

GERD HARDER | Intense (P)

CHARR CRAIL | I'm Sick Of Blonde Jokes (P)

THOMAS ROUSE | Body Wrap (P)

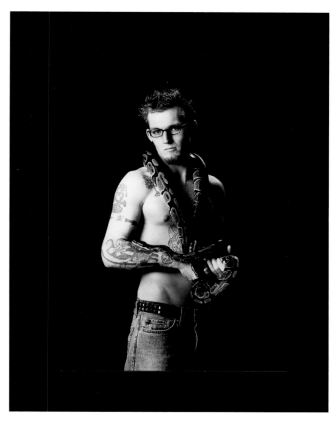

DARRIN HILL | Every Mother's Dream (P)

CARESSE MUIR | Sick Life (P)

LOAN COLLECTION

JON READ | Emerald Express (P)

MATTHEW LUCAS | Denim And Rust (P)

DARRELL CHITTY | America's Hymn Of Peace (P)

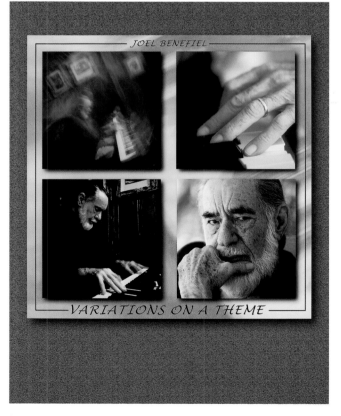

BOB COATES | Variations On A Theme CD Cover (P)

LOWELL TOOLE | Pelican Point (P)

WAYNE BELLING | Gondola Garage (P)

DAVE FOWLER | Etched In Stone (P)

SERENA PARENTE CHARLEBOIS | Widow's Walk (P)

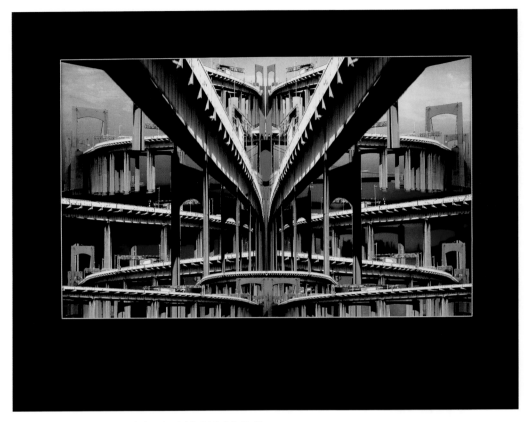

EDWARD J. MICHALEC | Steel-Linkage-In-Depth (P)

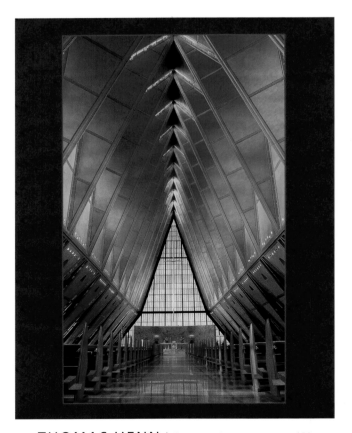

THOMAS HENN | Divine Inspiration (P)

DORAN WILSON | Red, White And Blue (P)

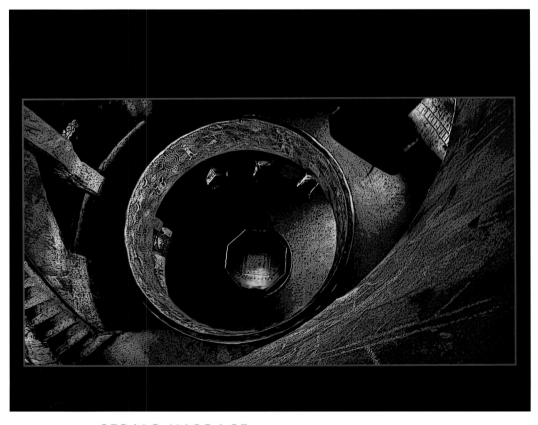

GERALD HARDAGE | Hay APAO - Power Of Air (P)

THOMAS ROUSE | The Dancer Within (P)

THOMAS ROUSE | Portrait In B Minor (P)

ANTHONY RUMLEY | Posing For The Gods (P)

WAYNE S. TARR | Stretched To The Limit (P)

ROBERT L. STEWART | Eagle Falls (P)

DANIEL THORNTON | String Lake (P)

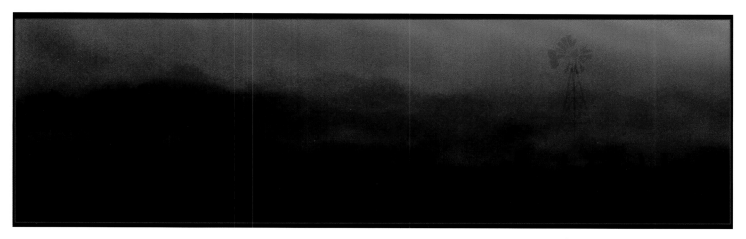

DWAINE HORTON | Misty Morning At The Ranch (P)

BEVAN WHITEAR | Crimson Dawn (P)

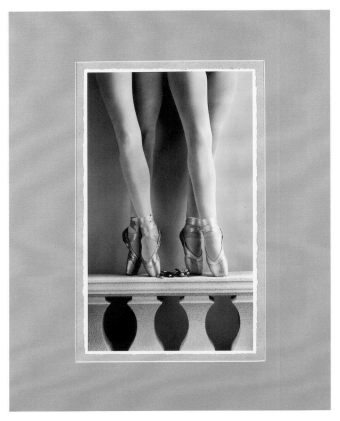

THERESA SMERUD | Duet (P)

RON FRANKLIN | On The Edge (P)

JAMES NELSON | Carter James (P)

SARAH RIVAS | Patient Eyes (P)

WAYNE BELLING | Heading Home (P)

DEBORAH BILLINGSLEY | Streets Of Provence (P)

RONALD NICHOLS | Serena (P)

DEBORAH FERRO | In Vogue (P)

DAVID COOPER | Mademoiselle (P)

SCOTT DUPRAS | The Jazz Man (P)

STEVE BEDELL | Flint (P)

YOUNG HWAN KANG | Joyful Elbow Wrestling (P)

JIM CARPENTER | Gotta Be Me (P)

TARRY CRUMLEY | Her Perspective (P)

BERT BEHNKE | Denim (P)

LOAN COLLECTION

THOMAS HENN | Synchronized Flight (P)

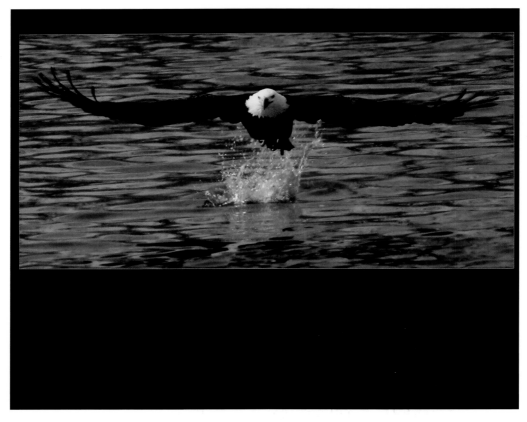

JESSE JOSLEYN | Raptor (P)

CHRIS LEGG | Texans On The Prowl (P)

JAMES P. CHAGARES | F-16 Fighting Falcons (P)

MARTY SIKES | The Bridge Less Traveled (P)

JOHN BLOYER | Going Their Own Way (P)

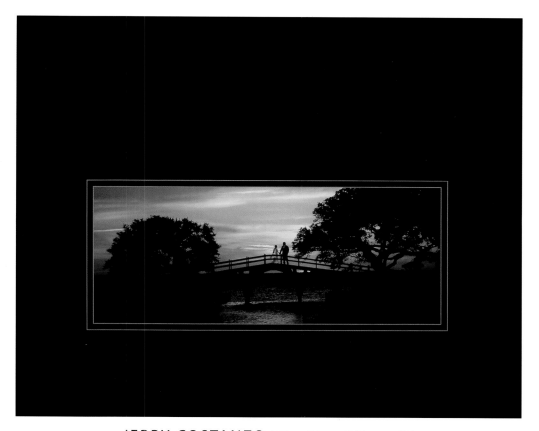

JERRY COSTANZO | The Glow Of Love (P)

DONG SEOK PARK | White Angels (P)

THEODORE SCARPINO | Sumac Rorschach (P)

TINA TIMMONS | Illusion (P)

LISA EVANS | Tapestry Of Art (P)

LISA EVANS | Autumn Stroll (P)

DENNIS HAMMON | Days Of Arthur (P)

PAUL CHRISTIAN | Night Run (P)

ROBERT KUNESH | Flight From Symmetry (P)

KEN WEBB | Breaking Free (P)

THOMAS ROUSE | The Muses Denied (P)

THOMAS ROUSE | The Body Electric (DP)

ROD BROWN | Sculptured By Time (P)

WILLARD SHATTUCK | For Thou Art With Me (P)

KAREN GOFORTH | Siren (P)

JAMES NELSON | Alicia's Eyes (P)

KENNETH SKLUTE | Commorant Fisherman (P)

JAMES FERRARA | The Gondolier (P)

ROBERT L. WILLIAMS | Misssion Bells (P)

TERRY MEADE | A Break In The Storm (P)

JACK HOLOWITZ | Rain Forest (P)

DENNIS HAMMON | Twisted By Time (P)

MARK GARBER | Little Boy Blue (P)

BETH FORESTER | Me And My Dad (P)

LOAN COLLECTION

POLLY CRUMLEY | Lavender (P)

BRAD LAMB | Did I Do Something Wrong (P)

HYUN MO HAN | Eye Contact (P)

CINDY ROMANO | Forever And Always (P)

BRANDON MICHAEL | Never Alone (P)

ALLEN D. MORTENSEN | Soothing Serenade (P)

HEATHER MICHELLE BJOERSHOL | Not A Girl, Not Yet A Woman (A-EI)

LORI SMITH | Salvaged Tintype (DP)

DANIEL THORNTON | Grand View (P)

DARTON DRAKE | Celtic Dream (P)

JON BUSHARD | Heartfelt (P)

JACKLYN PATTERSON | Gentleman And Scholar (P)

RICK AVALOS | Artist In Residence (P)

ROBERT L. STEWART | High And Dry (P)

KENNETH SKLUTE | Clearing Storm (P)

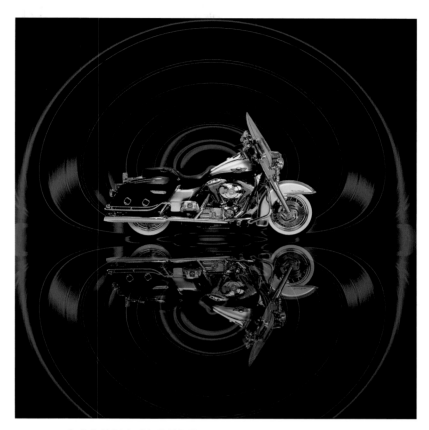

ROBERT CLEERE | 100 Years Of Rumble (P)

JOSHUA KANE | Driving Rain (P)

RHONDA WILKS | Someday (P)

MIRIAM HAUGEN | No Lambs At School (P)

GABRIEL ALONSO | Lassie Come Home (P)

BEVERLY MICHEL | It's All About Me (P)

LOAN COLLECTION

STEVEN AHRENS | On Deck (P)

BRAD CROOKS | Tunnel Vision (P)

PAULA MIGNOGNO | The Next Big Step (P)

RANDY MCNEILLY | Cosmopolitan (P)

RALPH ROOKEY | Elevator Out Of Service (P)

MEG CEBULA | Bridge To Another Dimension (P)

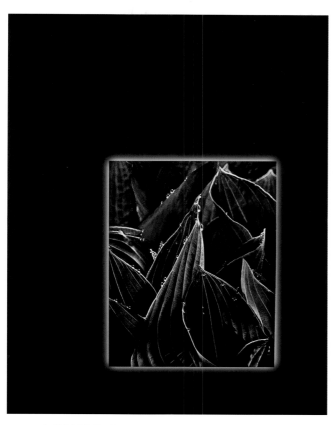

LOUISE SUPPLE | Morning Dew (P)

SCOTT WALZ | Designs In Emerald (P)

CHRIS BELTRAMI | Grandpa's Tractor (P)

SHERRON SHEPPARD | Waiting Out The Storm (P)

ANDREW JENKINS | On Top Of The World (P)

DENNIS WELLS | A Reflection Of Beauty (P)

ROD BROWN | Ancient Lands (P)

ANTHONY PATRICK MADDALONI | Geographical Flag Of America (P)

DANIEL THORNTON | Serpentine (P)

DANIEL THORNTON | Sandscape (P)

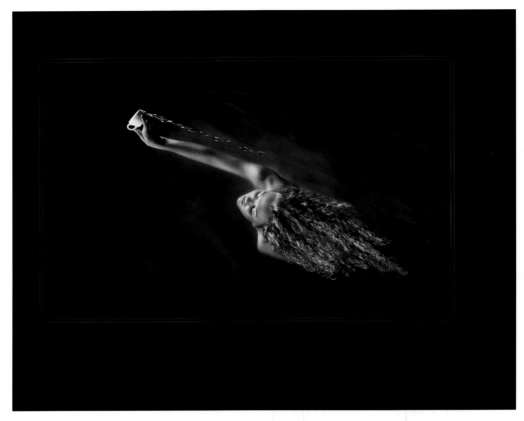

CRAIG KIENAST | Drink Offering (P)

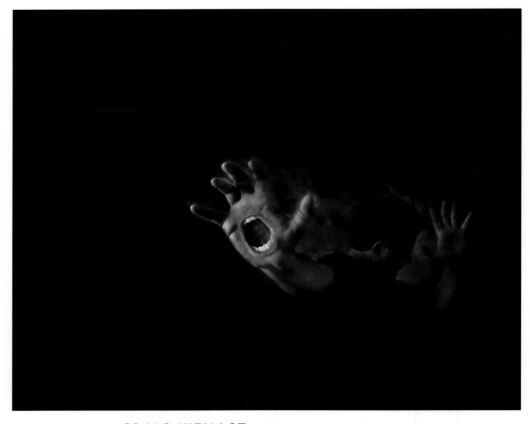

CRAIG KIENAST | Closed Angry Minds (P)

ERIC HINDERS | Reading Railroad (P)

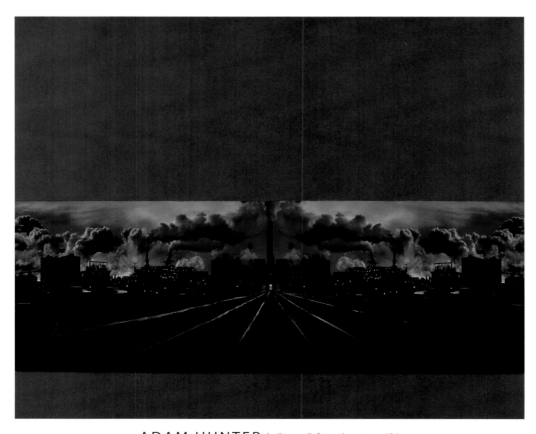

ADAM HUNTER | City Of Industry (P)

The Final Tip

NBA Finals Game 5
June 15th, 2004

ANDREW JENKINS | Final Tip (P)

DOUG GIFFORD | Bowman With His Hands Full (P)

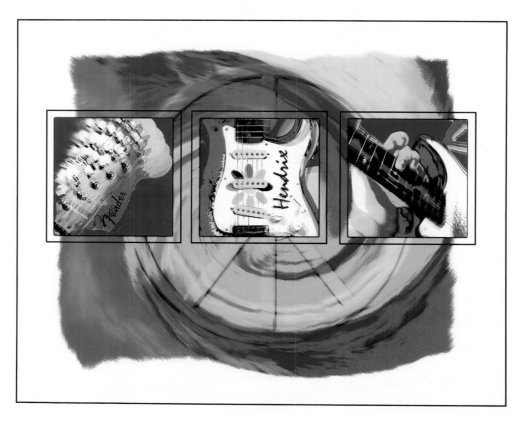

MARK A. WEBER | Psychedelic (P)

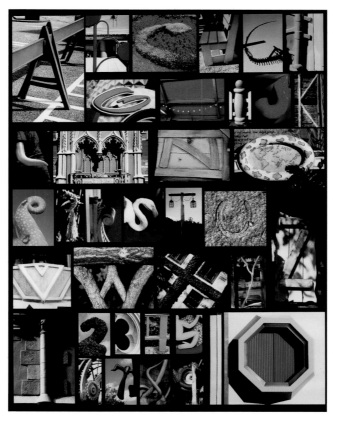

BRYAN WHITE | Disney ABC 123 (P)

DEBORAH KREIMBORG | Sydney (P)

BEVERLY TOVES | Second Thoughts (P)

ERIC JOHN BRUN | Swept Away (P)

JAE NAM LEE | Plighted Lovers (P)

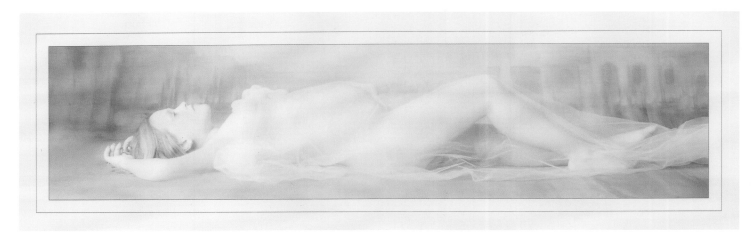

ANDREW JENKINS | Softly Defined (P)

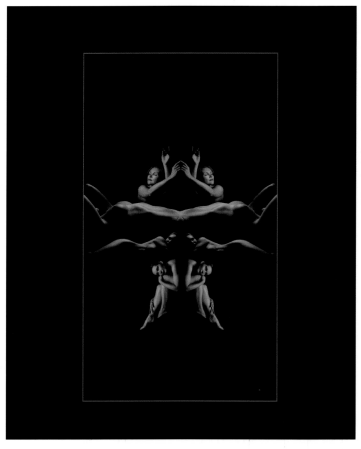

BETH FORESTER | Beautiful Creature (P)

95

JOHN GLADMAN | Legendary (DP)

BRET WADE | School Of Rock (P)

ESTHER BEITZEL | Simplicity (A-EI)

JO BURKHARDT | Romance Roman Style (A-EI)

JO BURKHARDT | Age Of Innocence (A-EI)

Base Image

ROBERT KUNESH | Coming Together (A-EI)

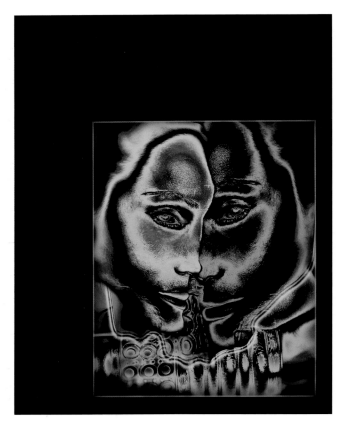

GERALDINE LAGO | Troubled Souls (P)

ROBERT KUNESH | Hard Drive Of Time (DP)

BUDDY STEWART | Highball (P)

TOM MCDONALD | The Last Mule Farmer (P)

BARARA VALLOT | Dressed To Be Blessed (P)

ROBERT HAWKINS | The Life I've Lived (P)

JAMES ZEILAN | The Sole Man (P)

MICHAEL TAYLOR | Mr. Whithers Witness To History (P)

ALAN MAYER | Tide Pools Of The Desert (P)

ALAN MAYER | Rapid Transit (P)

PETER LIK | Ancient Spirit (P)

CLAYTON SIBLEY | Evening Storm Over Navaho Country (P)

CHARLES ROUSE | A Point Of View (P)

STEPHANIE L. LAGOW | Laven Tanal (P)

RALPH ROOKEY | Down & Out (P)

BRAD CROOKS | Light Speed (P)

DENISE WINE | Tell Me A Story Please (P)

PATRICIA BELTRAMI | A Little Shy (P)

MARY GUELLER | In my Daughter's Eyes (P)

SHANNON KAYE LEDFORD | Sheltered (P)

MICHAEL FOX | Creeping Creation (P)

TAD D. MEDDAUGH | Handcrafted (P)

CANDACE YOUNG | Predator (P)

OSCAR LOZOYA | Proposicion De La Muerte (P)

PATRICIA BELTRAMI | Tuscan Monastary (P)

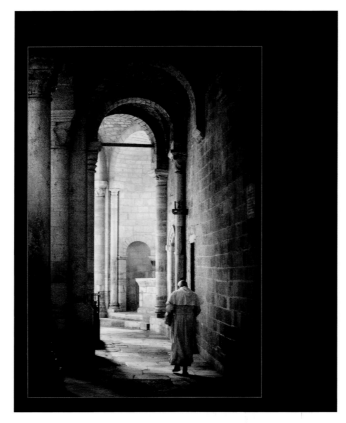

PAUL BLASER | Following The Light (P)

LOAN COLLECTION

JENNIFER HUDSON | Deliver Us From Evil (P)

CHRIS BELTRAMI | Time Marches On (P)

TIM OSTERMEYER | A Splash Of Autumn (P)

STAN JONES | Glade Creek Mill (P)

TODD ROYAL HICKEN | Out To Lunch (P)

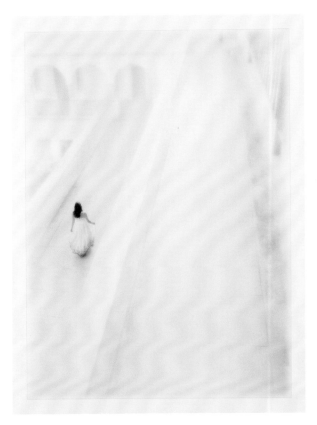

CARL CAYLOR |Walk Away (P)

CARL CAYLOR | Irish Cream (P)

SUN MI MOON | Beauty (P)

JENNIFER GILMAN | Enchantment (P)

MICHAEL TIMMONS | Winter's Blanket (P)

PAUL F. McMILLIAN | Winter Solitude (P)

DAVID HUNTSMAN | Winter In The Bluegrass (P)

GARY FAGAN | A Sleigh Ride Home (P)

JAMES CHURCHILL | Ice Man (P)

MICHAEL LAMM | Yer Out! (P)

LOAN COLLECTION

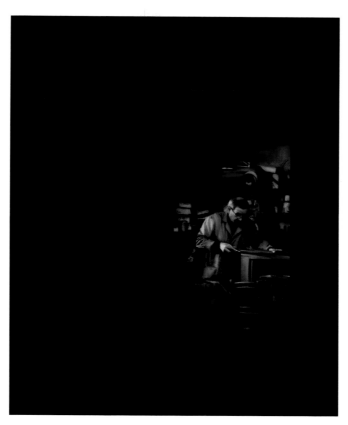

HEIDI HARDY | Handcrafted (P)

JAMES GARBER | Totem Carver (P)

LOAN COLLECTION

RHONDA WILKS | Pure Of Heart (P)

JULIE KLAASMEYER | Barely Bashful (P)

KWANG HYUN YOO | Bride 1 (P)

MARC PARRONE | Family Heirlooms (P)

HUD ANDREWS | Flower Fantasies (P)

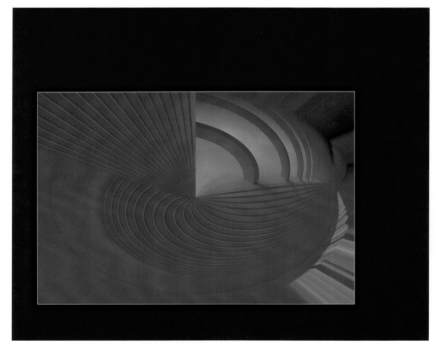

PAUL OWEN | Nautilus (P)

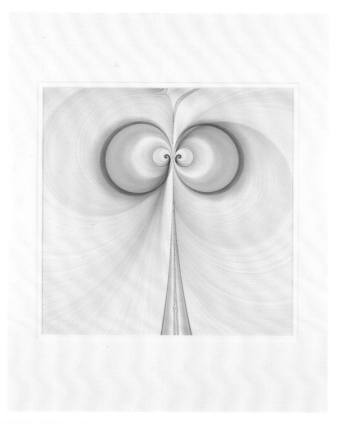

ROBERT HUGHES | Fractured Fractal Flower Factory (DP)

ROBERT CLEERE |Empurial Enchantment (P)

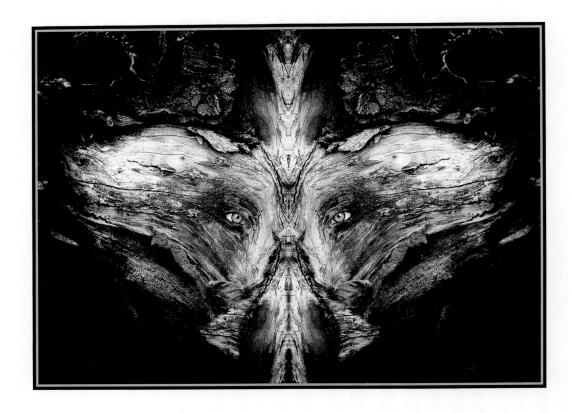

ROBERT KUNESH | Awakening (P)

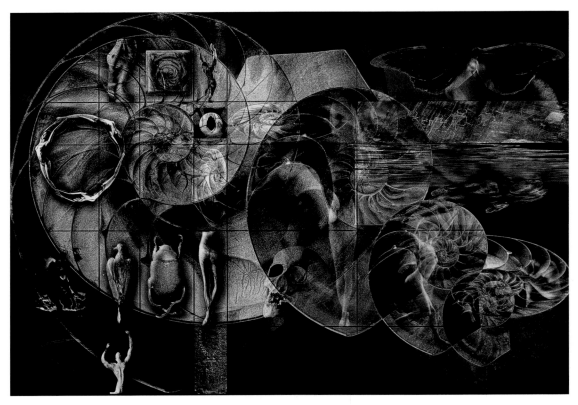

THOMAS ROUSE | A Natural History (P)

MARK A. WEBER | 5 String Thing (P) ·

DON CHICK | From The Darkness (P)

LORI GRICE | Tranquil Dreams (P)

ALEXANDRA COLLINS | Pearl (P)

CARL CAYLOR | Classical Breeze (P)

DARTON DRAKE | Cotton Candy Girl (P)

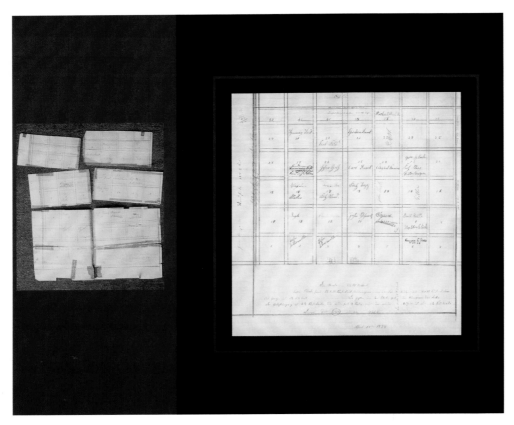

SUZANNE WALCOTT | 1879 Cemetery Plat (P)

JEAN MARIE POLAND | Hold Very Still (P)

BRUCE VAN PELT | The Labyrinth (DP)

CRAIG MINIELLY | Concrete Craftsman (C)

ELAINE HUGHES | Using The Can (P)

SEUNG HYU BAEK | Funny (P)

tri•Pod

BEVAN WHITEAR | Tripod (C)

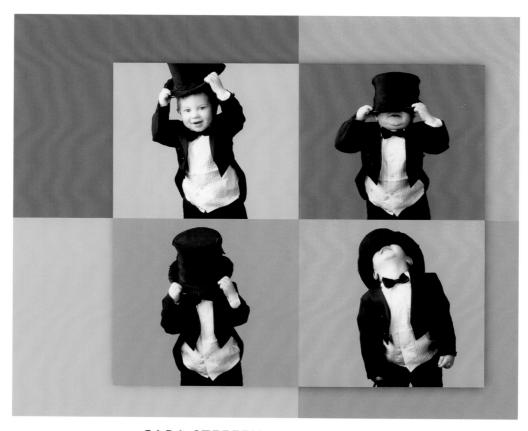

CARA STEFFEN | My Little Ham (P)

PATTY GEIST | Silent Watch (P)

SUZANNE FISCHER | Early Morning Warm-Up (P)

MARK CAMPBELL | Do Not Disturb (P)

DIXIE LAVAL | That's My Baby (P)

STEVEN AHRENS | A Shoulder To Lean On (P)

KAREN RUBIN | One Plus Two (P)

LOAN COLLECTION

DEANNE BUSATH PARRY | Les Petite Amies (P)

DENISE BRUNS | The Next Dance (P)

ANN NAUGHER | Quality Time (P)

DEBRA DeFAZIO | Kissed By A Rose (P)

IRENE BENAVENTE | Royal Tulip (P)

LOAN COLLECTION

HEIDI HARDY | Green With Ivy (P)

TAD D. MEDDAUGH | Alias (P)

MELISSA FORTENBERY | This Town Is So Dull (P)

GREGORY FINNEY | Ollie's Art (P)

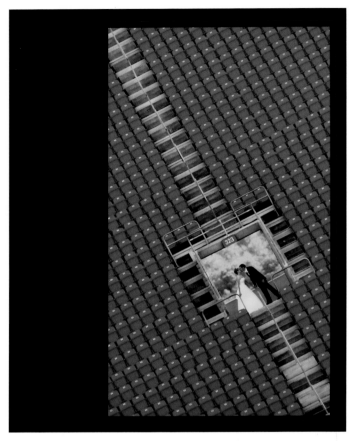

STEVE WILLIAMS | The Field Is Closed (P)

JAMES W. BYRON | I'm Gonna Miss Him (P)

JOHN TANNOCK | Foul Weather Friends (P)

GORDON O'BRIEN | Wedding Stroll (P)

DON CHICK | Needlework (P)

ROB BUCKMAN | Gearhead (P)

KAREN GOFORTH | Just As I Am (P)

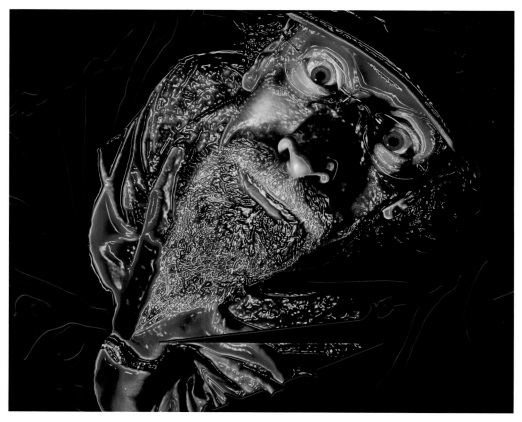

KRISH KIEFER | Ice Man (P)

GERD HARDER | Lady Of Solitude (P)

TONY HOPMAN | Captured (P)

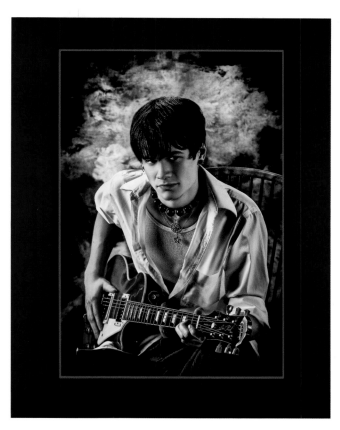

ALLEN D. MORTENSEN | Rocker (P)

JOHN GLADMAN | Blues Brothers (DP)

ROBERT CLEERE | Lost In A Maze (P)

JAMES P. CHAGARES | Dragon Tamer (DP)

DARTON DRAKE | Prophet (P)

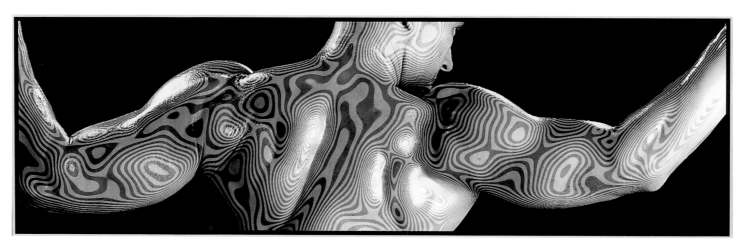

LORI GRICE | Moiréed And Morphed (P)

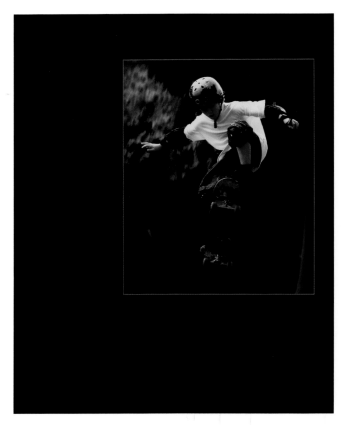

RANDY DAVIS | Hang Time (P)

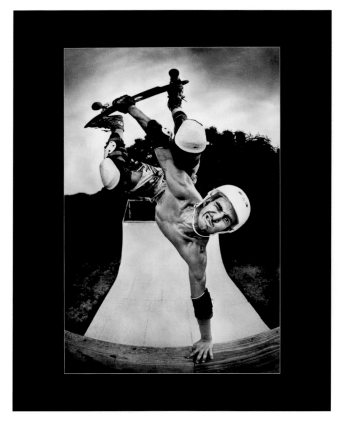

RICHARD PEZZIMENTI | Practicing For Perfection (P)

JAMES GARBER | I Eats Me Spinach (P)

CHRISTINE REYNOLDS | A Memorable Guest For Rent (C)

WENDY NEWMAN | The World Is Our Sandbox (P)

KATHLEENE FALLS | Singin' In The Rain (P)

WILLIAM BRANSON III | Shroud Of Innocence (P)

HELEN YANCY | Grandma's Wedding Dress (P)

JIM CHAMBERLAIN | Metaphysical Woman (P)

NANCY WOOD | Geometry (P)

LOAN COLLECTION

JAMES HAYES | Encircled (P)

DON RAUPP | Ice Angel (P)

SHANE GREENE | It's All About Attitude (P)

MARY JO ALLEN | Street Talkin' (P)

GERALDINE LAGO | Gangster-Fashion (P)

SCOTT GLOGER | Ray Of Hope (P)

STEVE ERVIN | Metaphysical Moscow (P)

LOAN COLLECTION

A. MACK SAWYER | Down And Out (P)

STEVE ERVIN | The Shepherd's Wife (P)

STEVEN HENRIQUES | Iron Maiden (P)

MICHELLE MADSEN CHILDERS | Secret Passage (P)

THOMAS ROUSE | Portrait In Time (DP)

JOHN WACKER | Modern Artist (P)

LOAN COLLECTION

TIM LARSEN-COLLINGE | Dawn Dreamer (P)

PAUL SMITH | Aloha Sunset (P)

VINCENT VITALE | Dawn Patrol (P)

JOHN MURRAY | September Solitude (P)

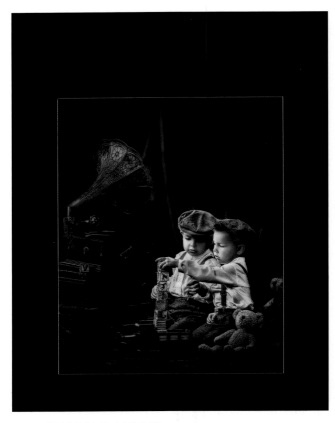

CINDY BAXTER | Building Bonds (P)

SCOTT DUPRAS | The Dreamer (P)

MICHAEL SKERRY | Joy (P)

JEFFREY DACHOWSKI | Nana's Dream (P)

BARRY RANKIN | Slapshot (P)

BARRY RANKIN | Fumble (P)

JESSE JOSLEYN | Burning Up The Track (P)

RALPH ROOKEY | Follow The Leader (P)

CANDACE YOUNG | Metamorphosis (P)

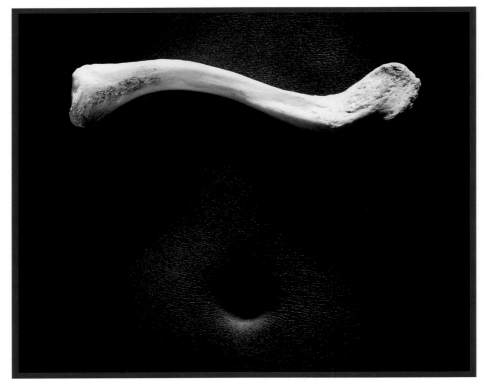

DAVID BAYLES | Inside Out (P)

JASON SMITH | Solar Steel (P)

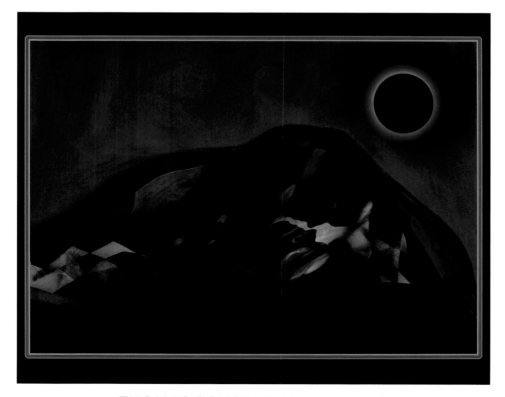

THOMAS ROUSE | Hidden Desire (DP)

DAVID COOPER | Hangtime (P)

JEFF DYER | Bending Birches (P)

OSCAR LOZOYA | We Have Each Other (P)

JULIE GUTWEIN | Where Has My Daddy Gone? (P)

YOSHINORI HAYASHI | Red And White (P)

KAZUO WATANABE | 20th Memory (P)

ISAM OTSUKA | Classic Elegance (P)

KAZUO WATANABE | 20th Anniversary (P)

AARON PATTERSON | Can I Get Up Now? (P)

ROGER CAREY | The Eyes Of Haiti's Future (P)

PEPITO | Faces Of Hope (P)

GRAHAM WILSON | Three Hearts, One Soul (P)

ANDY ANDREWS | Early Surfer (P)

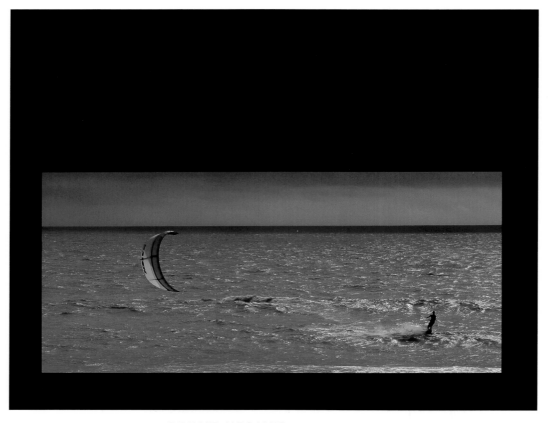

BRENT KEPNER | Blue Day (P)

JAMES HAYES | New Horizons (P)

JONG HUN PARK | Calm Of The Storm (P)

MARK SPENCER | Dizzy Dancing (P)

KWAN SUB SHIM | Amazement (P)

STEVEN NISSLE | Family Bonds (P)

MANUEL CRUZ | 50th Anniversary (P)

SUNNY CARREL | Roscoe And Renee (P)

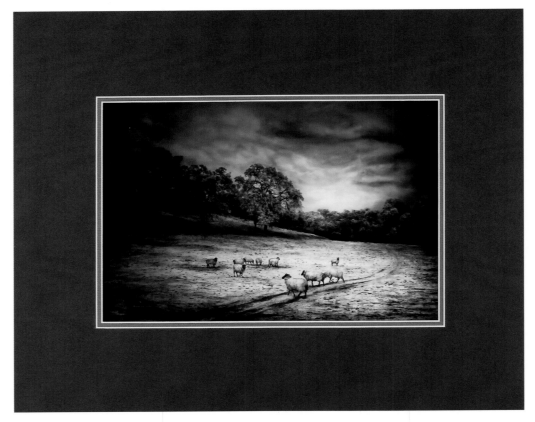

SHERRON SHEPPARD | A Simple Life (P)

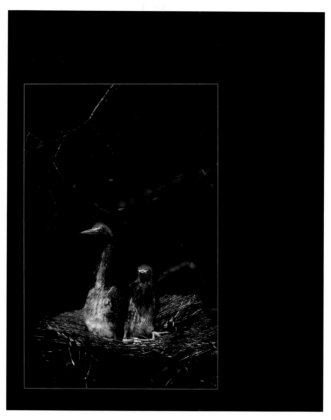

DON DAIGREPONT | Born On The Bayou (P)

MIYASAKA YOSHITOMI | Vertical Thrust (P)

DAVID SWOBODA | Going To Town (P)

RICHARD BEITZEL | The Traveler (P)

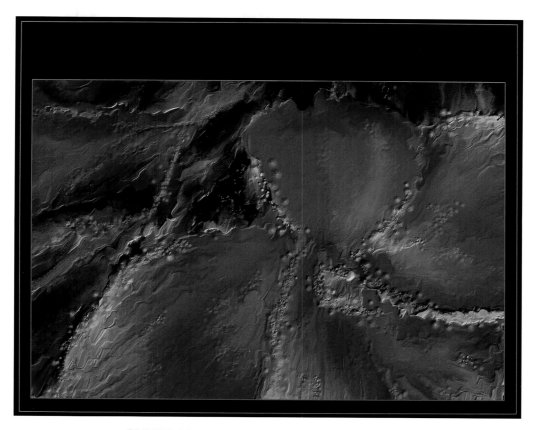

CHERI MacCALLUM | Red In Bloom (DP)

RICHARD GAFFNEY | La Vase (P)

SEUNG HO KANG | Graceful Pose (P)

SIN WOONG YOO | Elegance (P)

STEPHEN ABBOTT | Lovers Balcony (P)

JOSEPHINE A. SCHOEPFER | Breathless With Adoration (P)

MARK A. WEBER | Tail Gunner (P)

WOODY WALTERS | Born In The USA (P)

GIGI CLARK | Altered States (P)

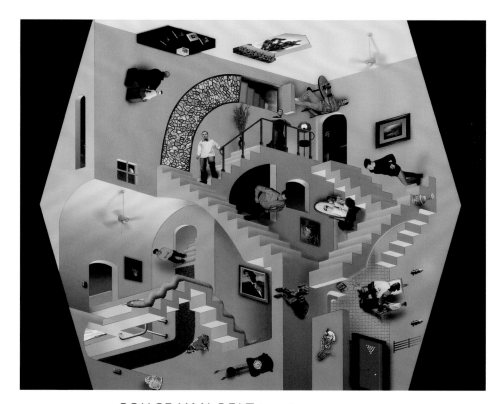

BRUCE VAN PELT | Escher-esque (DP)

MARTI WEIS | Winter Morn' (P)

KEVIN JIMINEZ | Morning In Jackson Valley (P)

DAVID HUNTSMAN | Road To Nowhere (P)

H. FRED COCKRILL | Frozen Pastures (P)

SE DONG KIM | A Pair Of Lovers (P)

TIMOTHY HAUGH | The Ocean's Chamber Of Love (P)

LOAN COLLECTION

BRUCE BELLING | Suburban Life — 2 Kids And A Dog (P)

KAREN B. KELLEY | Little Bridges (P)

LOAN COLLECTION

JOANN MUNOZ | Newborn Love (P)

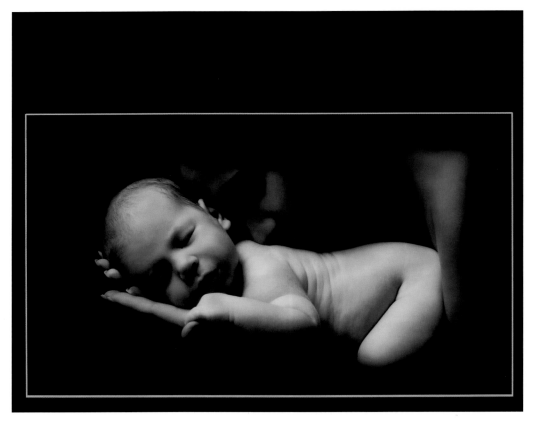

CHERILYN NOCERA | Sweet Dreams (P)

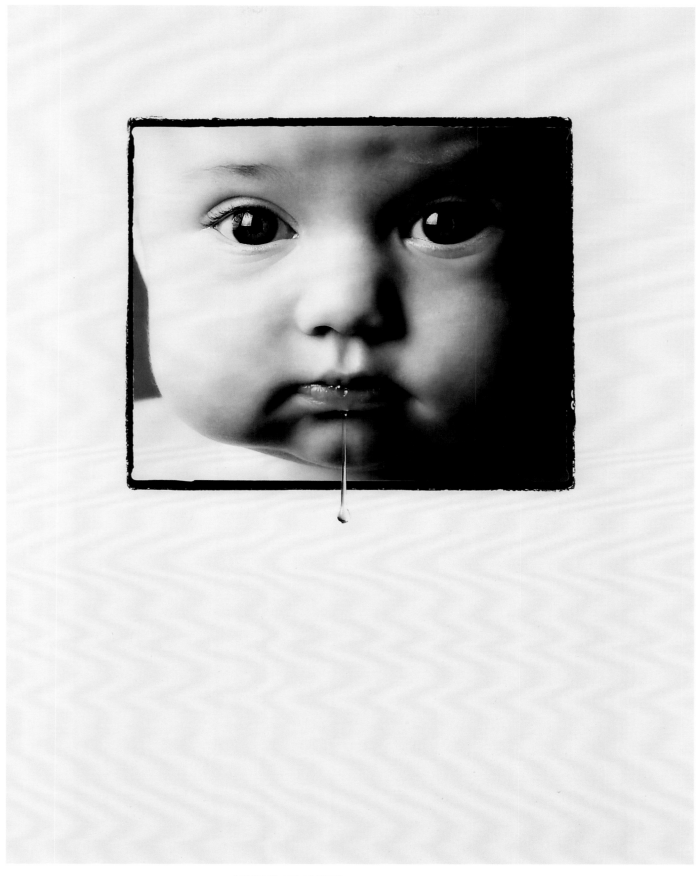

VICKI TAUFER | Spit Happens (P)

LOAN COLLECTION

RICHARD PEZZIMENTI | Family's Favorite Retreat (P)

KENNETH WHITMIRE | Lazy Afternoon (P)

TAMMY JOLLEY | Tuscan Sunset (P)

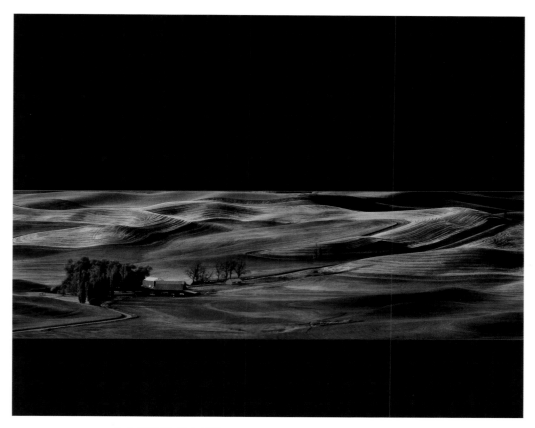

RANDY ZACK | "S" Curve To The Red Barn (P)

LOAN COLLECTION

CHRIS JOHN ROCKAFELLOW | Aqua Marine (P)

ROBERT L. WILLIAMS | Serenity Bay (P)

MICHAEL NICHOLS | Tranquil Harbor (P)

MICHELLE WILBUR | Mystic Point (P)

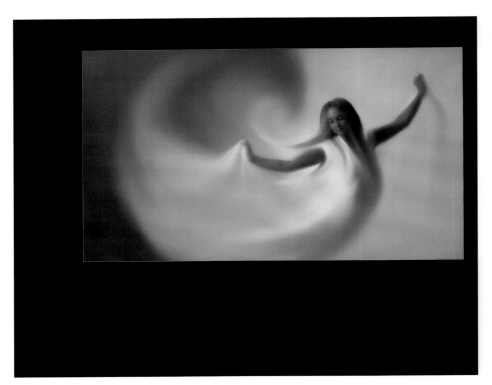

GREGORY E. LEHR | Feel the Air (P)

KRISH KIEFER | Spirit Dance (P)

JENNIFER HUDSON | The Light Of Love (P)

JENNIFER HUDSON | The Visionary (P)

JAMES W. BYRON | Mr. Washington (P)

STEPHEN PEECK | Grandpa (P)

KERRY BRETT HURLEY | The Journey Begins (P)

TOM EGENES | Circle Of Life (P)

DORAN WILSON | Low Tide (P)

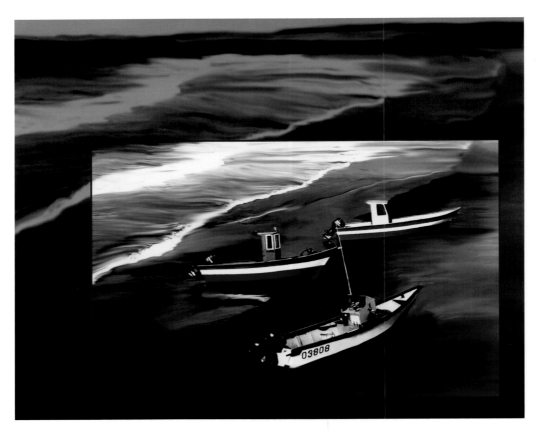

CAROLYN TERRY | Ah Shore (P)

STEVE JESSEE | Netscape (P)

DENNIS CRAFT | San Juan Puerto Rico (P)

DANIEL DAVIS | Victoria (P)

CAROL ANN DWYER | Hindu Princess (P)

JAYNE ERICKSON | Hear My Prayer (P)

ZERIHUN BEZABEH | Vision Of Mystery (P)

RICK BELCHER | After The Kill (P)

TIM OSTERMEYER | Vanishing Freedom (P)

BRUCE VAN PELT | Albino Kingsnake (P)

KENNETH BOVAT | Pond Perfect (P)

STEVEN WHITE | Emerging Day (P)

SHERRON SHEPPARD | First Light (P)

ALLEN BRADLEY HAWKS | Tranquility (P)

STEVEN KEMP | Safe Haven (P)

JAMES STAGNER | Curves (P)

MARTY SIKES | Purple Passion (P)

SUNNY CARREL | Chateau Bordeaux (C)

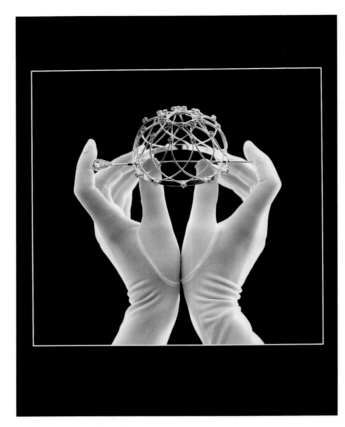

DANIEL DOKE | Grace (P)

JAMES FERRARA | Waiting To Be Wed (P)

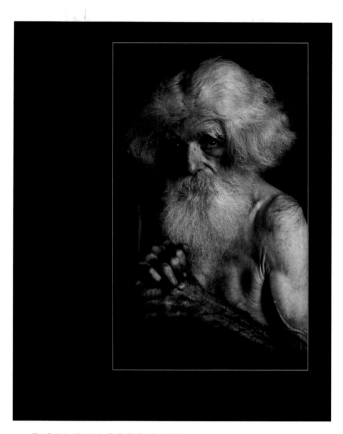

DON DAIGREPONT | Forgotten Soul (P)

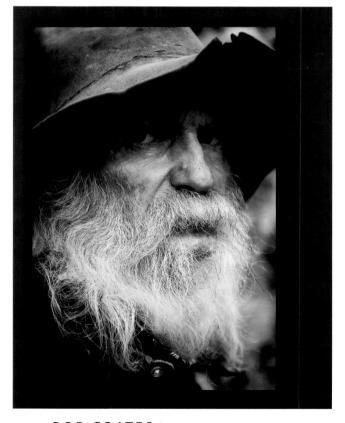

BOB COATES | Vanishing Breed (P)

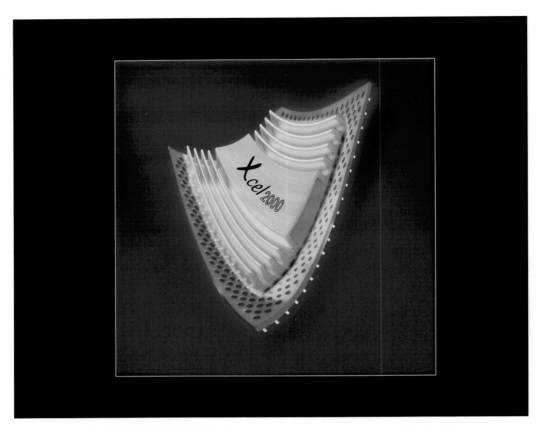

DORAN WILSON | Flexible Computing Heat SYNC (P)

SUSAN B. CECIL | The Year Of The Dragon (P)

SUZANNE FISCHER | Corvette Classic (C)

JAMES P. CHAGARES | Game Over (P)

LYLE OKIHARA | Nocturnal Neon (P)

CHARR CRAIL | The Guttermouth Drummer (P)

TERRY MEADE | Preflight Inspection (P)

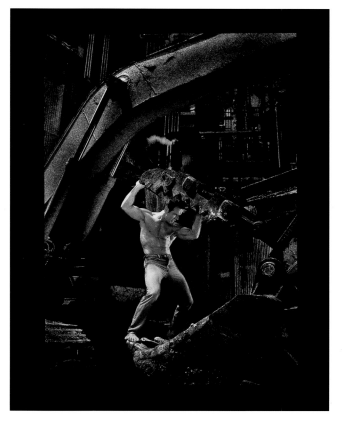

MICHELLE MADSEN CHILDERS | Rage Against The Machine (P)

JOHN WACKER | Frosty Morning (P)

MICHAEL A. TRAVISANO | Early Winter's Morning (P)

THOMAS HENN | Aging Gracefully (P)

DWAINE HORTON | Dust In The Wind (DP)

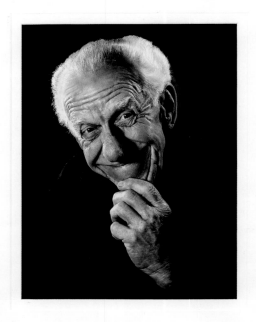

JAMES GARBER | I'm Just Tickled Pink (P)

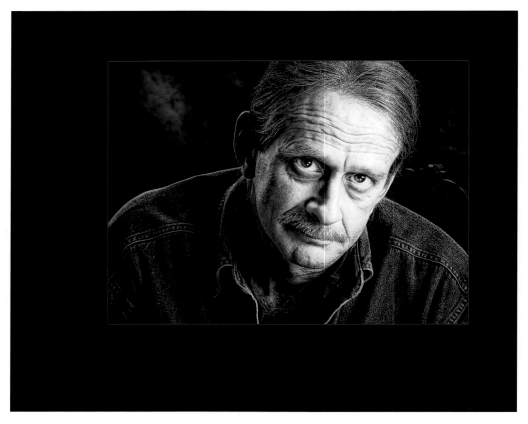

DON CHICK | Weathered By Choices (P)

DEBORAH RUYMEN | Going Crazy (P)

LARRY LOURCEY | The Commuter (P)

KARIE HAMILTON | Nordstrom Shopper (P)

PATRICK BATES | Mosaic Beauty (P)

BOGDAN FUNDALINSKI | The Birth Of The Galaxies (P)

PATRICIA MATHIS | Metamorphosis (P)

CRAIG KIENAST | Sullen Veil (P)

GERALD HARDAGE | London Morn' (P)

KEITH MILLS | Winter Wonderland (P)

ANN NAUGHER | Snow Angels (P)

GORDON O'BRIEN | Sisters (P)

JOHN RIDGEWAY | A Wondering Moment (P)

ANN NAUGHER | Hat Dance (P)

KATHRYN MEEK | Colors Of The Caribbean (P)

CHRIS BELTRAMI | Our Town (P)

LAURA MOUL | Morning Path (P)

MICHAEL WADE | Misty Morning Sunrise (P)

CARL CAYLOR | Wrinkled In My Drawers (P)

JANET BOSCHKER | Cutie Patootie (P)

MICHAEL SKERRY | Flower Child (P)

KATHY WIERDA | Last Minute Details (P)

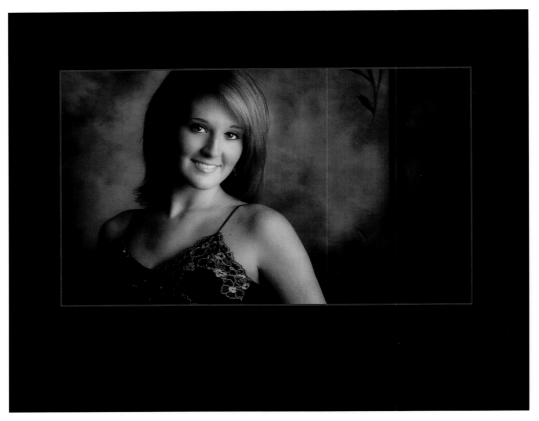

JENNIFER ENGLERT | Claire (P)

SEUNG HO KANG | Classical Beauty (P)

JONG HUN PARK | A Frosty Morning (P)

SEUNG HO KANG | Charming Lady (P)

JAMES FRIEZE | Morning Flight (P)

ROSE MARY HENDERSHOT | Swan Lake (P)

VINCENT VITALE | Prairie Sentinel (P)

CARRELL GRIGSBY | Autumn Flight (P)

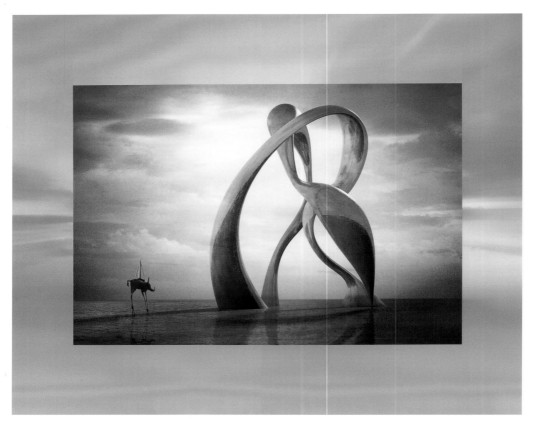

STEPHEN HARTMAN | Dream Of The Pink Elephant (P)

ERIC HINDERS | The Elephant (P)

JEFF KAISER | Leader Of The Pack (P)

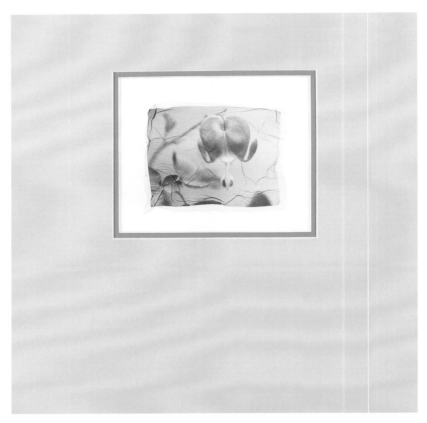

J. MICHAEL McBRIDE | Solitary Heart (P)

GARY PHILLIPS | Heart Of The Matter (P)

PEGGY HATFIELD | Petal Dance (P)

MARY JO ALLEN | Dahlia Burst (P)

RICHARD PEZZIMENTI | Sun Kissed (P)

SANA ANTISDEL | Behind Closed Doors (P)

PETER BURG | Hot Lips (P)

JON PETERSEN | Transformation (P)

KEN WEBB | Sweet Otis (P)

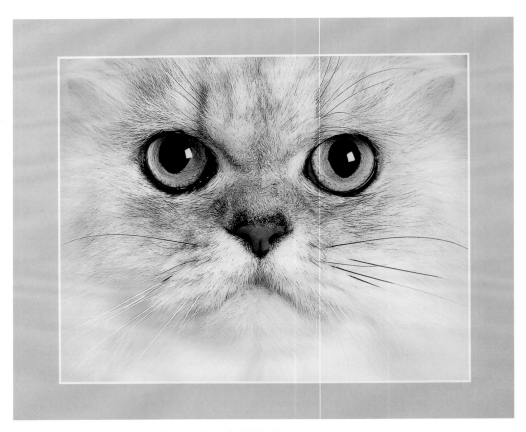

MICHAEL JOSEPH | Let's Face It (P)

TRICIA BRUNNER | Left Behind (P)

LOU SZOKE | The Springer Septuplets (P)

ARLEEN THOMAS | Solitude (P)

TIMOTHY HAUGH | Twilight Calm (P)

MARK CAMPBELL | Sunrise Stroll (P)

TIMOTHY MATHIESEN | Ocean Sunset (P)

JEFFREY JACOBS | Convention Center Lobby (C)

JEFFREY JACOBS | Performing Tonight (C)

JEFFREY JACOBS | Company's Coming (C)

ERIC JOHN BRUN | Enchanted Forest (P)

JACK HOLOWITZ | Forest Glen (P)

ERNIE K. JOHNSON | Sentinel By The Sea (P)

MICKEY GINN | Alcazar (P)

DANIEL DAVIS | Anna Lee (P)

MARY ANNE McATEE | Mystic Morning (P)

MARK KIEFER | Femme Zupan (P)

KAREN B. KELLEY | Winter Blue (P)

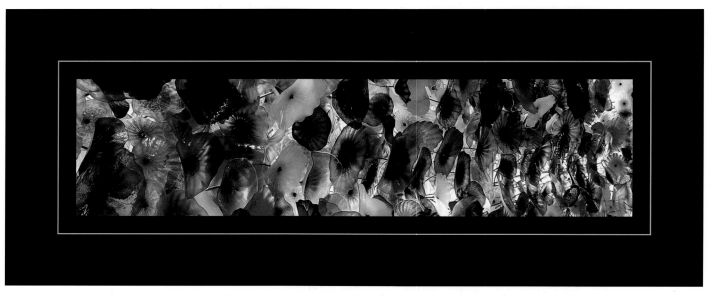

LORI GRICE | Glass Garden (P)

GAIL NOGLE | Giselle Age 4 (P)

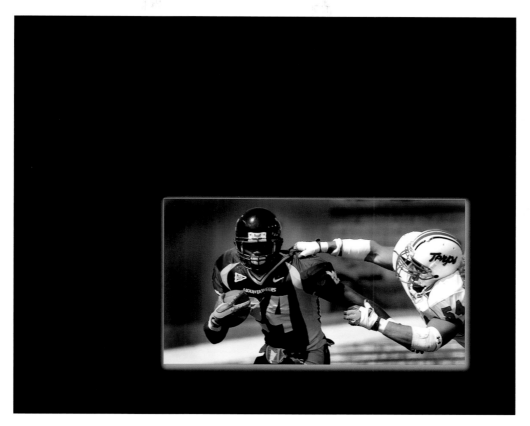

BRENT KEPNER | Gotcha (P)

BARBARA VALLOT | Can't Wait 'Til Quittin' Time (P)

ALBUMS

HEATHER KALLHOFF And DAVID L. GRUPA | Just As My Heart Imagined (AM)

KIMBERLY SAYRE | Jeff And Michelle (AM)

PAUL ROGERS And DAVE ACEVEDO | Two Hearts, One Love (AM)

STEWART POWERS And SUSAN POWERS | Jenny And Michael (AM)

JENNIFER GILMAN And MARK GARBER | A Perfect Summer Day (AM)

MARK GARBER And JENNIFER GILMAN | The Art Of Love (AM)

LORI NORDSTROM | "Two" (A)

LORI NORDSTROM | Expecting Elijah (A)

ANN NAUGHER | Brittany's First Day Of Kindergarten (A)

MELISA SMOCK | Fairy Tale Tea Party (A)

BETSY LYN BUTLER | Shayna And Derek (A)

GAIL DeMARCO | Tahoe Album (A)

SHERRI EBERT | Once Upon A Time In Mexico (A)

JOHN WRIGHTENBERRY | We Did It Our Way (A)

ANGELA TALENTINO-RAMOS And JENNIFER ENGLERT | Eowyn And Matthew (AM)

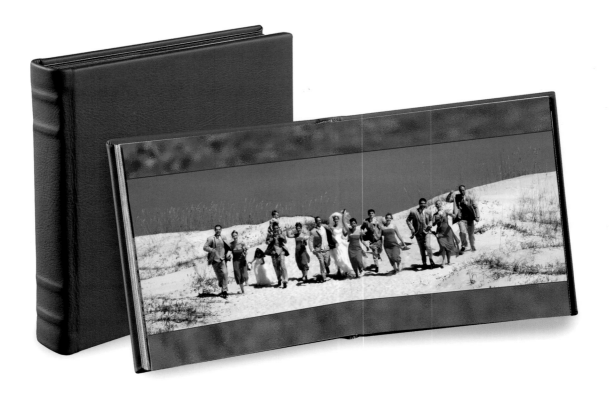

BRENDA ESTES And STEVEN ESTES | Tiffany And Alan (AM)

ALLISON ENGLISH WATKINS | Natalie And Walter (A)

J. WIECZOREK | To Live, To Laugh, To Love (A)

AMANDA ENGEL | A Day In The Life Of Grover Lamont (A)

LOAN COLLECTION INDEX

LOAN COLLECTION INDEX

CATEGORY CODES

PHOTOGRAPHIC

P — Photographic
C — Commercial / Industrial
S — Scientific / Technical
A — Album

ART / TECH

A — Photographic Artist
A-E/I — Artist, Electronic Imaging
NR — Negative Retoucher

ELECTRONIC IMAGING

V/SE — Video, Special Effects
V/CCI — Video, Commercial/Corporate/Industrial
DP — Digital Print
DT — Digital Transparency
D/RE — Digital, Retouching/Enhancement

LOAN COLLECTION

2005 International Jurors

JURY CHAIRS

Hud Andrews
Dennis Craft
James Frieze
Mark Garber
Robert Golding
David Huntsman
Tim Mathiesen
Duncan McNab
Warren Motts
Barry Rankin
Ralph Romaguera
William Stevenson
Buddy Stewart
Michael Taylor
Bill Weaks
Helen Yancy

JURORS

Jon Allyn
Dori Arnold
Jon Blom
Rod Brown
Debbie Chagares
Jim Chagares
Kaye Frey
Patty Geist
Joan Genest
Doug Gifford
Dennis Hammon
Robert Hawkins
Kalen Henderson
Keith Howe
Stephen Lagow
Lee Larsen

JURORS

Rex Lavoie
J. Michael McBride
Randy McNeilly
Richard Newell
Ron Nichols
Aaron Pepis
Paul Tishm
Linda Weaver
Greg Wurtzler
Robert Zettler